English - Pashto bilingual dictionary contains over 400 words in the following categories: home, health, body, numbers, clothes, food, senses, weather and colors.

Next to every page, there is place for practicing your hand writing. There are also some pages left at the end if you need more space.

This book is perfect to learn the language for adults and for kids.

Please rate us on Amazon. It's very important for us and for other customers.

HOUSE - کور
(KOR)

WINDOW - کړکۍ
(KARHKIE)

ROOF - چت
(CHAT)

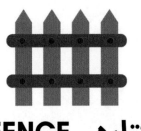

FENCE - کتاره
(KATARA)

CHIMNEY - دودکښ
(DODKAZH)

DOOR - دروازه
(DARWAZA)

TERRACE - برانده
(BARANDA)

SHED - شید
(SHAID)

ROOF TILE - د چتټایل
(DA CHAT TAYEL)

GATE - ور
(WUR)

GUTTER - لښتی دناولو اوبو
DA NAWALU UBU LAKHTI)

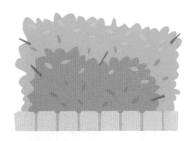

HEDGE - انګر
(ANGARH)

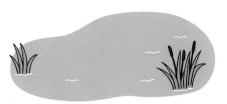

POND - حوض
(HAUZ)

FEEDER - خوړک ورکونکي
(KHWARAK WERKAUNKY)

FLOWERS -
ګلونه
(GOLONA)

LAWN - چمن
(CHAMAN)

WATERING CANE -
اوبهورکولوګنی
(OBAWARKWALOGANRHI)

TREE HOUSE - د ونوکور
(DA WANOKO)

LAWNMOWER - چمن دريبالو مشين
(DA WAKHO REBALO MASHEN)

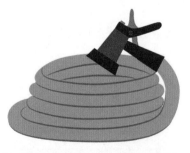

GARDEN HOSE -
دباغ لپاره جراپي
(DA BAGH LAPARA JARAP

GARAGE - گاراج
(GARAJ)

GARDEN STORAGE-
د باغ ذخیره **(DA BAAGH ZAKHEERA)**

TRAMPOLINE –
ترامپولین
(TRAAMPOLEEN)

KENNEL FOR DOG -
دسپی کوډله
(DA SPEE KODLA)

MAILBOX - کونوبکس/لیک بکس
(DA LEKONO BAX/LEK BAX)

CURTAIN - پرده
(PARDA)

STAIRCASE - زینه
(ZEENA)

FIREPLACE - د اورځای
(DA ORR ZAYE)

LIFT - پورته کول
(PORTA KAWAL)

HEADPHONES - هيادفوني
(HEDFON)

TV REMOTE CONTROL
دتلویزیون ریموټ
(DA TALWEZON REMOTE)

SATELLITE ANTENNA –
سپوږمکی انتن
(SPOGMIEANTAN)

INTERCOM - ده اریکه
(GADA AREKA)

PHONE - تيلفون
(TALEFON)

TV - تلویزیون
(TALWEZON)

CHANDELIER - قندیل
(CANDEL)

SWITCH - سویچ
(SWECH)

RADIO - راډیو
(RAADYO)

LOUDSPEAKERS –
غږ جګی
(SPEKARONA)

RUG - غالی (GHALIE)

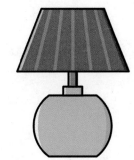

LAMP - څراغ (SERAGH)

ARMCHAIR - لاس لرونکی چوکی (LAS LARUNKY CHOWKIE)

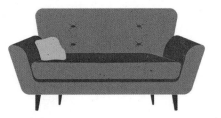

SOFA - نرمه چوکی (NARMA CHAWKI)

RADIATOR - ریډیټر (RADEETAR)

IMAGE - عکس (AKAS)

CUPBOARD - الماری (ALMARIE)

DRESSER - دپخلنځی میز (DA PAKHLANZI MEZ)

VASE - گلدان (GULDAN)

**KITCHEN - پخلنځی
(PAKHLANZAII)**

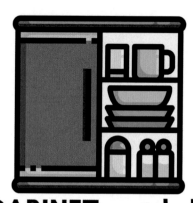

**CABINET - الماری
(ALMARI)**

**STOOL - سندلي
(SANDALI)**

**TABLETOP - د میزسر
(DA MAIZSAR)**

**COFFEE TABLE -
دقهوی میز
(DA KOHWY MEZ)**

**TABLE - میز
(MAIZ)**

**CHAIR - چوکۍ
(CHAWKI)**

**TRASH CAN -
کثافتدانی
(KASAFAAT DANI)**

**REFRIGERATOR
- یخچال
(YAKHCHAL)**

MORTAR - اونگ
(AWANG)

SINK - دست شوی
(DAST SHOI)

STOVE - دیگدان
(DEGDAN)

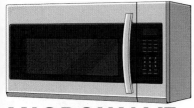

MICROWAVE - مایکروویو - (MICROWAVE)

PAN - کړایی
(KARAI)

NAPKINS - دسمال
(DUSMAL)

POT - لوښی
(LOKHEE)

CUTTING BOARD-
د پری کولو تخته
(DA PREKAWALO TAKHTA)

MUG - غټ ګلاس
(GHAT GALASS)

BLENDER – یو‎ډول دشیانو ګډونکی ماشین (YAW DAWAL DA SHIANU GADAWNKI MASHIN)

MIXER – مکسر (MIKSAR)

LADLE – اوړده کاچوغه (UZDA KACHUGHA)

ROLLING PIN– چوبه (CHUBA)

KETTLE – چایجوشه (CHAI JOSHA)

PLATES - غابونه (GHABUNA)

CUTLERY - غوثونکی آله (GHOSAWONKI AALA)

FORK - پنجه (PANJA)

GLASS - ګلاس (GALAAS)

CUP - پياله (PIYALA)

KNIFE - چاقو (CHAQO)

PEELER - پوستولو آله (POSTAWALO AALA)

TEASPOON - دچايو کاچوقه (DA CHAI KACHUKA)

SPOON - کاچوقه (KACHUKA)

**BEDROOM – د خوبخونه
(DA KHOBKHONA)**

**WARDROBE – کالو الماری
(DA KALO ALMAREE)**

**MIRROR – هنداره
(HINDARA)**

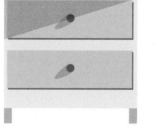

**BEDSIDE TABLE –
د دبستری دڅنگ میز
(DA BESTAR DA SÁNG MEZ)**

**FRAME PHOTO –
دعکس چوکات
(DA AKAS CHOKAT)**

**BED – بستره
(BESTARA)**

TOYBOX -
د لوبودشیانو بکس
(DA LOBO DA SHIANU BAKS)

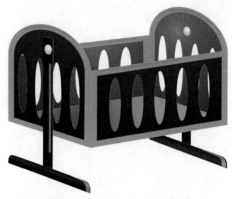

زانګو – CRADLE
(ZANGO)

دبدلولومیز – CHANGING TABLE
(DA BADLAWALU MEZ)

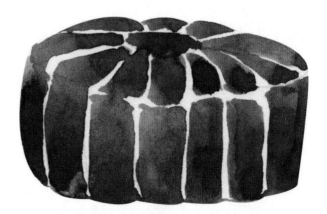

پوف . – POUFFE
(POOF)

OFFICE CHAIR – ددفترمیز
(DA DAFTAR MEZ)

BATHROOM – تشناب (TASHNAAB)

SHOWER – شاور (SHAWAR)

TOILET – تشناب (TASHNAAB)

WASHING MACHINE – د کالووینگلومشین (DA KALO VENZALO)

SOAP – صابون (SABOON)

TOILET PAPER تشناب کاغذ (TASHNAAB KAGHAZ)

HAIRDRYER – وینبتانوچونکی (WEKHTANWACHONKI)

BATH – حمام (HAMAM)

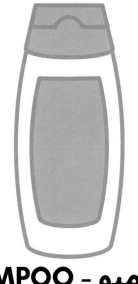

COMB - رمونز (ZHAMANZ)

HAIRBRUSH - دويبنتانوبرس (DA WEKHTONO BARS)

HAMPOO - شامپو (SHAMPOO)

TOWEL - تول (TWAL)

TOOTHBRUSH- دغانبوبرس (DA GHAKHONO BARS)

TOOTHPASTE - دغانبونوكريم (DA GHAKHON KREM)

BODY - بدن
(BADAN)

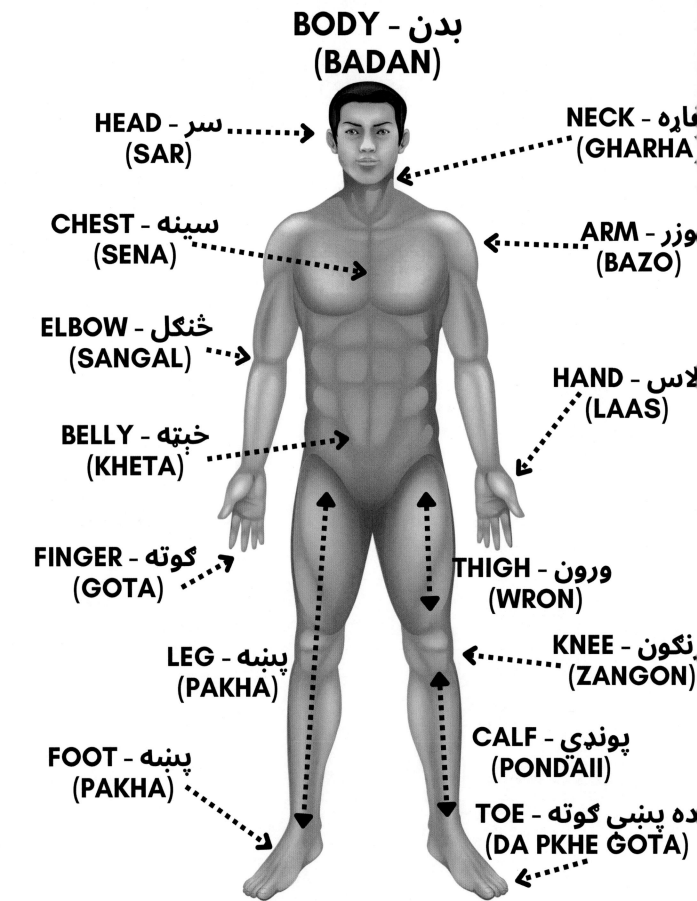

HEAD - سر
(SAR)

CHEST - سینه
(SENA)

ELBOW - څنګل
(SANGAL)

BELLY - خېټه
(KHETA)

FINGER - ګوته
(GOTA)

LEG - پنبه
(PAKHA)

FOOT - پنبه
(PAKHA)

NECK - ماره
(GHARHA)

ARM - وزر
(BAZO)

HAND - لاس
(LAAS)

THIGH - ورون
(WRON)

KNEE - نګون
(ZANGON)

CALF - پوندي
(PONDAII)

TOE - ده پنبی ګوته
(DA PKHE GOTA)

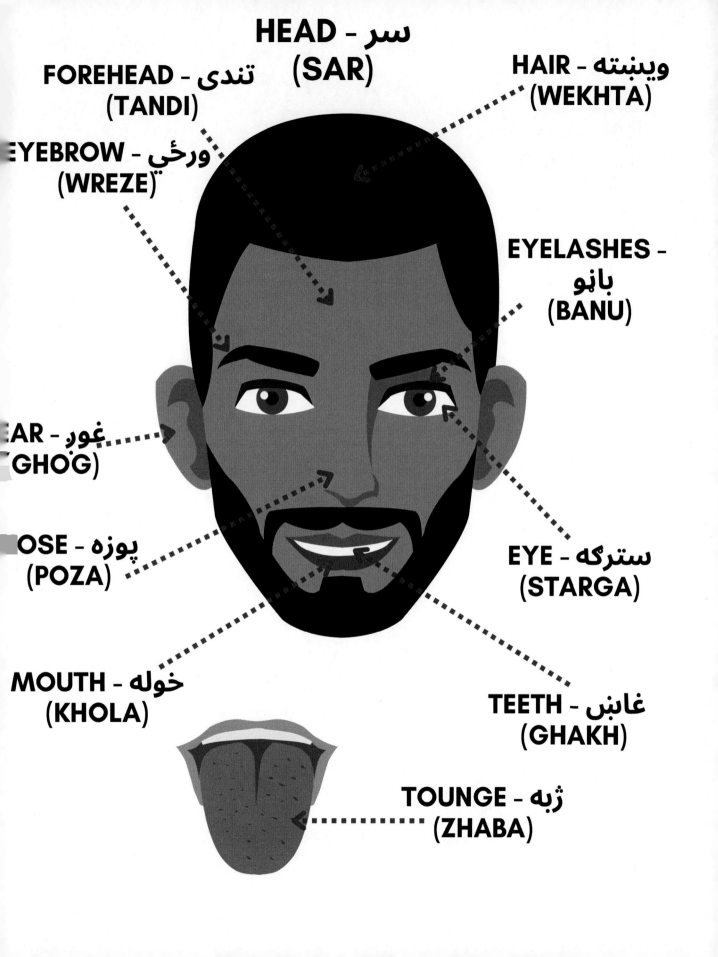

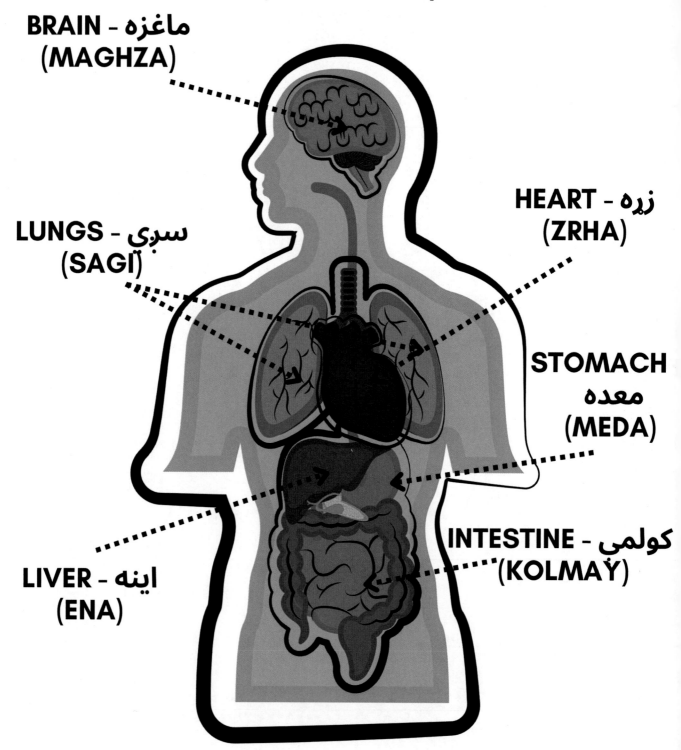

ANATOMY - اناتومي
(ANATOME)

BRAIN - ماغزه
(MAGHZA)

HEART - زره
(ZRHA)

LUNGS - سږي
(SAGI)

STOMACH
معده
(MEDA)

INTESTINE - کولمی
(KOLMAÝ)

LIVER - اینه
(ENA)

SENSES - حسكول (HASS KOL)

**SIGHT - ديد
(DEED)**

**SMELL - بويول
(BOYEWAL)**

**TASTE - ثكل
(SAKAL)**

**TOUCH - لمس
(LAMAS)**

**HEARING - اوريبدل
(AWREDAL)**

ADJECTIVES - اناتومي

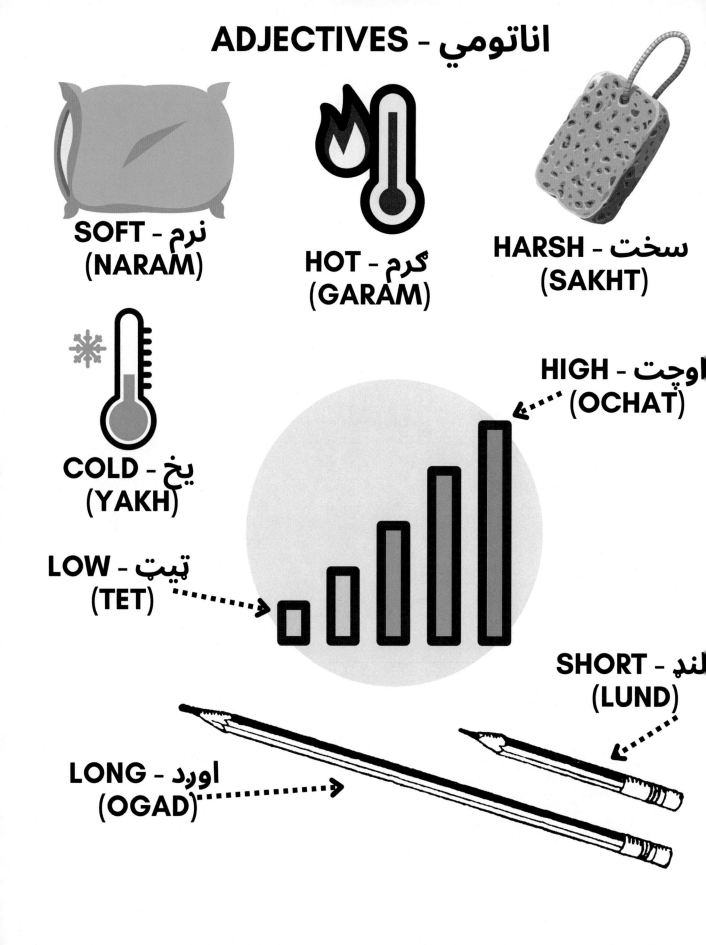

SOFT - نرم
(NARAM)

HOT - گرم
(GARAM)

HARSH - سخت
(SAKHT)

COLD - يخ
(YAKH)

HIGH - اوچت
(OCHAT)

LOW - تيت
(TET)

SHORT - لند
(LUND)

LONG - اورد
(OGAD)

SMALL - وروکی
(WARHÖKE)

BIG - لویی
(LOOYE)

SOUR - تریخ
(TREW)

SWEET - خوږ
(KHOOĠ)

SALTY - مالګین
(MALGEEN)

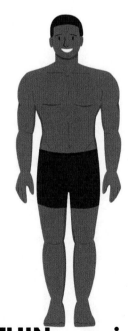

FAT - چاغ
(CHAGH)

THIN - نری
(NARAÏI)

BITTER - ترش/تریو
(TURSH/TRIU)

**DRY - وچ
(WACH)**

NEAR - نرِدې

**WET - خیشت
(KHESHT)**

**FAR - لیری
(LARÄY)**

**QUIET - خاموش
(KHAMOOSH)**

**LOUD - اوچت
(OCHATT)**

EMOTIONS - احساسات
(EHSASAT)

JOY - خوښي
(KHWASHEE)

SADNESS - خپگان
(KHAPGAN)

FEAR - ویره
(VERA)

ANGER - غوسه
(GHOSSA)

SHAME - شرم
(SHARAM)

BOREDOM - ستریا
(STARHYA)

HEALTH AND HYGIENE – روغتیااوحفظالصحه (ROGHTYA AW HIFZULSIHHA)

COUGH – ټوخی (TOKHEE)

FEVER – تبه (TABA)

PILS – ګولۍ (GOLIE)

RUNNY NOSE – بهبدونکیپوزه (BAHEDONKE POZA)

BANDAGE – بنداژ (BANDAZH)

PLASTER - پلستر
(PLASTAR)

WOUND - زخم
(ZAKHAM)

SYRUP - شربت
(SHARBAT)

THERMOMETER - ترمامیتر
(TARMAMETAR)

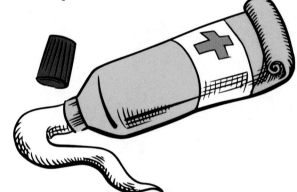

OINTMENT - ملهم
(MALHAM)

BRUSH - برس
(BARS)

SPONGE - سپنج
(SPANJ)

NAIL CLIPPER-
ناخونگیر
(NOKHUN GIR)

SHAPES - شكلونه (SHAKLONA)

TRIANGLE - مثلث (MUSALLAS)

RECTANGLE - مستطيل (MUSTATEEL)

DIAMOND - الماس (ALMAS)

CIRCLE- دايره (DAIRA)

TRAPEZOID - دوهارخيزه (DWAARHKHEZ)

DIAMOND - الماس (ALMAS)

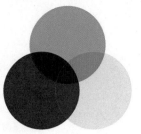

COLOUR - رنگونه (RANGONA)

YELLOW - زیر (ZYER)

BLUE - شین/آسمانی (SHIN/ASMANI)

RED - سور (SOOR)

VIOLET - بنفشه (BANAFSHA)

ORANGE - نارنجی (NARANJE)

GREEN - شین (SHEEN)

BROWN - نصواري (NASWARI)

WHITE - سپین (SPEEN)

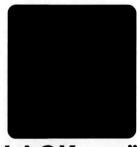

BLACK - تور (TOOR)

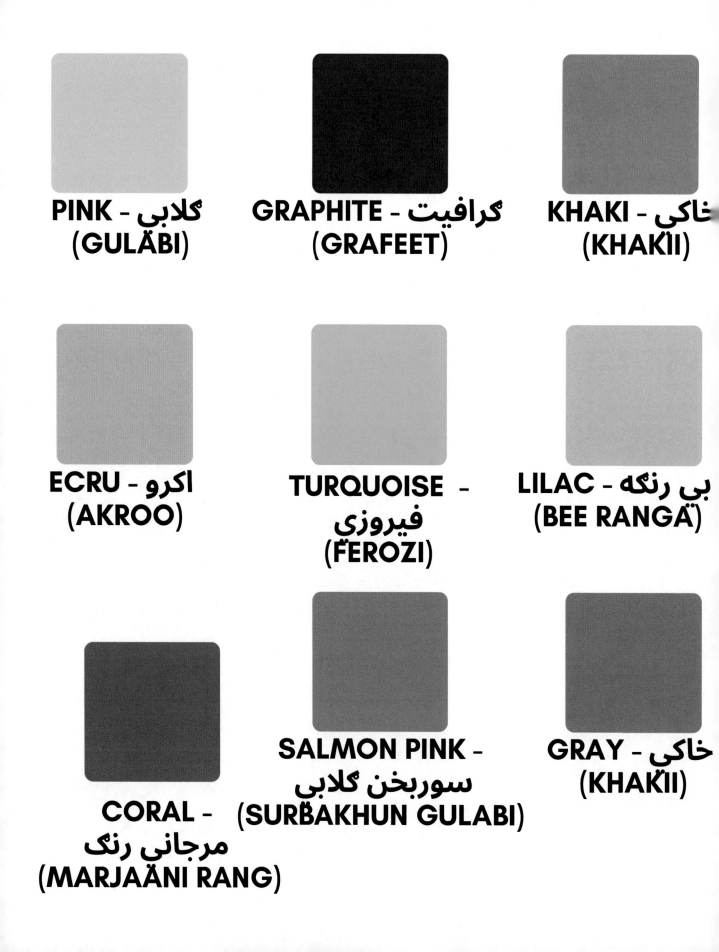

PINK - گلابی
(GULĂBI)

GRAPHITE - کرافیت
(GRAFEET)

KHAKI - خاکی
(KHAKÌI)

ECRU - اکرو
(AKROO)

TURQUOISE - فیروزی
(FEROZI)

LILAC - بی رنگه
(BEE RANGA)

CORAL - مرجانی رنگ
(MARJAĂNI RANG)

SALMON PINK - سوربخن گلابی
(SURBAKHUN GULABI)

GRAY - خاکی
(KHAKÌI)

CLOTHES AND ACCESSORIES - جامې او لوازم
(JAMAY AW LAWAZEM)

BRA - نیکر/پتلون لنډ - **SOCKS** - جرابی
(LAND PATLUN/NEKAR) (JURABAY)

LEGGINGS -
پتاواپاینچی
(ATAWAPAINCHE)

KNEE SOCKS -
ترزنګون پوری جرابی
(TAR ZANGON PORI JAMI)

PANTS - پتلون
(PATLON)

TIGHTS -
تنګیجامی
(TANGAIJAMAI)

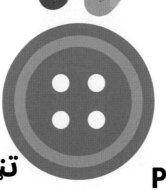

BUTTON - تڼی
(TANRHI)

PANTIES - لنډی جامی
(LANDI JAMEE)

SKIRT - لمن
(LAMAN)

DRESS - جامى
(JAMÁI)

HAT - خولى
(KHOLIE)

CAP - توپى
(TOPIE)

SWEATER - انګيا
(ANGIA)

T-SHIRTS -
لند لستونى والا كميس
(LAND LASTONI WAL
KAMIS)

SCARF -
سكارف
(SKARF)

HEADSCARF -
دسردسمال
(DA SAR DUSMAL)

SHORTS - لندېجامى
(LANDAYJAMÁI)

SANDALS - چوتۍ (CHAWATI)

GLOVES - دستکشی (DASTAKSHE)

JACKET - جیکټ (JEKAT)

HOODIE - دکوټ خولۍ (DA KOT KHUWALI)

SUIT - جوړه کالۍ (JORA KALI)

SNOW BOOTS - د واورېبوټان (DA WAWRAYBOOTAN)

RAINCOAT - دهبارانکوټ (DA BARANKOT)

SWIMSUIT - دلامبوکالۍ (DA LAMBO KALI)

COAT - کوټ
(KOT)

SLIPPERS - چپل
(CHAPAL)

PAJAMA -
پاجامه/پرتوګ
(PAJAMA/PARTUG)

BATHROBE -
د حمام چپنه
(DA HAMAM
CHAPANA)

TRAINERS - روزونکی
(ROZONKIE)

BELT - کمربند
(KAMARBAND)

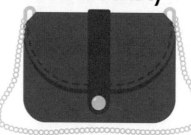

CLUTCH BAG -
کلچکثوړه د
DA KLACHKASORHA

HAIRPIN -
دهويښنبتوستن
(DA WEKHTO)

TOP - پورتهجامی
(PORTA JAMAI)

GLASSES - عینکی
(AINAKI)

SUSPENDER – تسمه
(TASMA)

BRACELET – بنگړی
(BANGRAI)

WATCH –
لاسی ساعت
(LASI SAAT)

EARRING – غوږوالی
(GHOGWALIĖ)

NIGHTDRESS –
دخوب جامي
(DAˈKHUB JAMAI)

NECKLACE –
هار/اميل
(HAAR/AMAIL)

BAG – کثوړه/بسته
(KASUNA/BASTA)

FRUIT - میوه
(MEWA)

NECTARINE -
کوچنی شفتالو
(KUCHNI SHAFTALU)

CRANBERRIES -
کرینبیری
(KRANBERRY)

VEGETABLE - سبزي
(SABZI)

WATERMELON -
هیندوانه
(HENDWANRHA)

شفتالو - PEACH
(SHAFTALOO)

BLUEBERRIES -
بلوبیری
(BLOWBERRY)

GOOSEBERRY -
غوزه (GHOOZA)

زردالو - APRICOT
(ZADALU)

**TRAWBERRIES -
خُمکنی توت
ZMAKANI TUT)**

**BANANA - کیله
(KELA)**

**کیوی – KIWI
(KEWI)**

**RASPBERRY -
توت ډوله میوه
TUT DAWLA MEWA)**

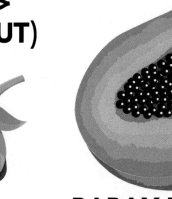

**پاپایه – PAPAYA
(PAPAYA)**

**GRAPES – انگور
(ANGOOR)**

**BLACKBERRY -
تور توت
(TOOR TUT)**

**COCONUT – کوپره
(KOOPRA)**

**CHERRIES -
ګیلاس
(GILAAS)**

APPLE – منه
(MANA)

PEAR – ناک
(NAAK)

MANDARIN – مندارین
(MANDAREEN)

PINEAPPLE –
اناس
(ANANAS)

LIME – ليمو
(LEMO)

PLUM – الوچه
(ALOOCHA)

LEMON – ليمو
(LEMO)

ORANGE – نارنج
(NARANJ)

**PASSION FRUITS -
شوقمیوه د
(DA SHAWQMEWA)**

**PAMELA - پامیلا
(PAMELA)**

**GGPLANT - بانجان
(BANJAN)**

**PUMPKIN - کدو
(KADDO)**

**MANGO - آم
(AAM)**

**MELON - ختکی
(KHATAKE)**

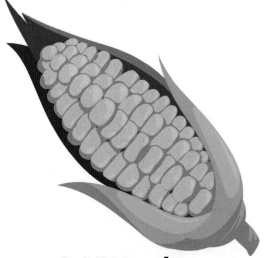

**CORN - جوار
(JAWAR)**

ONION – پیاز
(PEYAZ)

PEAS – نخود
(NAKHOD)

BEANS – لوبیا
(LOBYA)

ARTICHOKE –
آرتیچوک
(ARTECHOK)

PEPPER – تورمرچ
(TOORMRACH)

LETTUCE – کاهو
(KAHO)

LEEK – گندانه
(GANDANA)

TOMATO – سوربانجان
(SOORBANJAN)

CABBAGE – کرم
(KARAM)

CAULIFLOWER - (GOBEE) گوبی

BROCCOLI - گوپی (GOPEE)

کورجیټ - **COURGETTE** (KORJEET)

بادرنگ - **UCUMBER** (BADRAANG)

بروکسلسپروټس د - **BRUSSELS SPROUTS** (DA BORKSALSPRAWOOT)

چقندر - **BEETROOT** (CHAQANDAR)

گاجر - **CARROTS** (GAJAR)

POTATOES - الوگان/پتاتی (ALOGGAN/PATATEE)

مولی - **RADISH** (MOOLEE)

**BREAKFAST - ناشته
(NASHTA)**

**LUNCH - غرمهدودی
(DA GHARMAI DODIE)**

**CHEESE - پنیر
(PANEER)**

**YOGHURT - مستی
(MASTEE)**

**EGGS - هگی
(HAGIE)**

**DAIRY - لبنیات
(LABNIAT)**

**MILK - شیدی
(SHEDEY)**

**DINNER -
دهمابنامهدودی
(DA MAKHAM DODIE)**

**WHIPPED CREAM -
ویپشویکریم
(WEPSHWEKREEM)**

GRAIN PRODUCTS - د غنومحصولات (DA GHANAMOMAHSOOLAT)

COTTAGE CHEESE - کورنیپنیر (KORNEE PANEER)

FLOUR- اوړه (OWRHA)

BUTTER - کوچ (KOCH)

WHEAT BREAD - دهغنمودودی (DA GHANAMO DODIE)

BAGUETTE - بگوته (BAGOTA)

RICE - وریجی (WREJEY)

OAT FLAKES - دهاوربشپاوړه (DA ORBASHAIOWRHA)

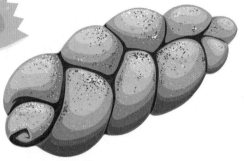

PASTA- پاسته (PASTA)

CHALLAH - ډوډۍ (DODI)

ROLL - وله ډوډي (LOLA DODI)

CROISSANT - کروسينټ (KROSENT)

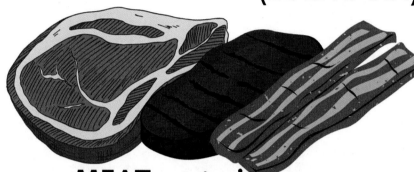

MEAT - غوښه (GHOKHA)

PATE - ککري (KAKARI)

CHICKEN - دچرګ غوښي (DA CHARGAH GHWAKHI)

SAUSAGE - پيچلی غوښه (PACHLE GHWAKHI)

SALAMI - دغوايي وچي غوښي (DA GHUWAYI WACHI GHWAKHI)

DESSERT - خواره
(KHWAGA)

HONEY - شات
(SHAAT)

MUFFIN - پسته کولچه
(PASTA KULCHA)

PIE - کباب
(KABAB)

WAFFLE - کولچه
(KULCHA)

ICE CREAM - ایسکریم
(AYES KREEM)

SALAD - سلاته
(SALATA)

DRINKS - خٹنباک (SAKHAK)

TEA - چای (CHAI)

COMPOTE - کمپوت (KAMPOT)

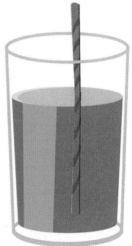

JUICE - جوس (JOOS)

LEMONADE - دهلیموشربت (DA LEMOSHARBAT)

HOT CHOCOLATE - گرمچاکلیټ (GARAMCHAKOLAT)

WATER - اوبه (OBA)

COFFEE - قهوه (KAHWA)

NUMBERS - شمېرې
(SHMERĖY)

**ONE - يو
(YO)**

**TWO - دوه
(DWA)**

**THREE - دري
(DRE)**

**FOUR - څلور
(SALOR)**

**FIVE - پنځه
(PENZA)**

**SIX - شپږ
(SHPĀG)**

**SEVEN - اووه
(OWA)**

**EIGHT - اته
(ATA)**

**NINE - نهه
(NAHA)**

**TEN - لس
(LAS)**

**ZERO - صفر
(SEFAR)**

COUPLE - جوړه
(JORHA)

EVEN - جفت
(JAFT)

LEFT - کیڼ
(KEENRH)

13579

ODD - طاق (TAAQ)

SECTION - برخه
(BARKHA)

LINE - کرښه (KARKHA)

POINT - ټکی
(TAKI)

RIGFT - ښی
(KHEE)

GROUP - ګروپ
(GROOP)

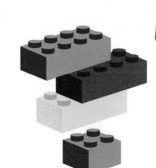

SET - مجموعه/سیټ
(MAJMOA/SET)

DOZEN - درزن
(DARZAN)

ME OF DAY - ورځنۍ وخت
(WRAZENAE WAKHT)

EVENING - ماښام
(MAKHAM)

NIGHT - شپه
(SHPA)

MORNING - سهار
(SAHAR)

SUNRISE - نمرخاته
(NAMARKHATA)

MOON - سپوږمۍ
(SPOGMÍE)

THE SUNSET -
دلمرلوېدل
(DA LEMAR LWEDAL)

SUN - نمر
(NAMAR)

DEW - نم/پرخه
(NAM/PARKHA)

STAR - ستوری
(STOREE)

WEATHER - موسم
(MOSAM)

CLOUD - وریځي
(WARYAZAI)

WAVES - څپي
(SAPE)

WIND - باد
(BAAD)

LIGHTENING - روښنايي
(ROKHNAII)

FLOOD - سیلاب
(SAILAB)

STORM - طوفان
(TOFAN)

FORECAST - وړاندوینه (WRHANDWENA)

FROST - شبنم (SHABNAM)

HEAT - تودوخه (TAWDAKHA)

HAIL - ژله (ZHALA)

SUNNY DAY - لمرينه ورځ (LEMARINA WRAZ)

HEAVY RAIN - تيز باران (TEEZ BARAN)

ALE - سخت طوفان (SAKHT TOFAN)

RAINBOW- شنهزرغونه (SHNA ZARGHONA)

TORNADO - بوربوکی (BORHBOKIE)

SEASON - فصل
(FASL)

SPRING - پسرلی
(PASARLE)

SUMMER - اوړی
(OWRHE)

WINTER - ژمی
(ZHAMII)

AUTUMN - مني
(MANII)

Made in the USA
Coppell, TX
12 October 2024

38567059R00031